WATERMELON MAN

Katie Donovan was born in 1962, and spent her early youth on a farm in Co. Wexford. She studied at Trinity College Dublin and at the University of California at Berkeley, and spent a year teaching English in Hungary. She now lives in Dublin where she works as a journalist with the *Irish Times*. She has published two collections, *Watermelon Man* (1993) and *Entering the Mare* (1997), both from Bloodaxe.

She is the author of *Irish Women Writers: Marginalised by Whom?* (Raven Arts Press, 1988), and has co-edited two anthologies: *Ireland's Women: Writings Past and Present* (with A. Norman Jeffares and Brendan Kennelly), published by Kyle Cathie (Britain), by Gill & Macmillan (Ireland) in 1994, and by Norton & Norton (USA) in 1996; and *Dublines* (with Brendan Kennelly), published by Bloodaxe in 1996

KATIE DONOVAN

Watermelon Man

BLOODAXE BOOKS

ISBN: 1 85224 215 9

First published 1993 by
Bloodaxe Books Ltd,
P.O. Box 1SN,
Newcastle upon Tyne NE99 1SN.

Second impression 1999.

Bloodaxe Books Ltd acknowledges
the financial assistance of Northern Arts.

Cover printing by J. Thomson Colour Printers Ltd, Glasgow.

Printed in Great Britain by
Bell & Bain Limited, Glasgow, Scotland.

For Phoebe Donovan

Acknowledgements

Acknowledgements are due to the editors of the following publications in which some of these poems first appeared: *Acorn, Authentik, Between the Circus and the Sewer* (Dublin Writers' Workshop, 1988), *Bitter Harvest* (Scribner's and Macmillan, New York, 1988), *Cyphers, Envoi, The Irish Press, Krino, Poetry Ireland Review, Poets Aloud Abú* (Ink Sculptors, 1988), *Raven Introductions 5* (Raven Arts Press, 1988), *Salmon, Shout* and *STET*. Some of these poems have also been broadcast by RTE Radio One in *The Poet's Chair*, and by BBC Radio 4 in *Stanza*. Thanks to the Tyrone Guthrie Centre at Annaghmakerrig where some of the work involved in this collection was carried out.

Contents

Making Terms: Sarospatak, Hungary, 1987-88

You Meet Yourself

You can get lost in America,
disappear from one coast
to another, the little lake
of childhood left behind,
bobbing with mementoes:
faces, nicknames, one-winged penguins,
the whiff of the candy store.

Then your head surfaces
on the crowded ocean of the new place,
you're another pebble on its beach,
clacking coldly against your fellows
on the tidal rhythm of rush hour.

Try that same voyage out in Ireland,
and you'll find yourself tripping
on your own umbilical cord;
forge ahead with a beefy crawl
and you'll hit a memory
at every stroke:
the grey brothers on the tide
transform into your old schoolmate,
your third cousin,
your neighbour's mother;

the shop down the road
is still there, and when you enter
your nose is haunted by the smell
of sweety biscuits and sliced pan –
the same immortal couple run the place;
the penguin sits behind your cupboard door
waiting to come alive at your opening;
the scarfed women still huddle on street corners
in corn-careful crêpe boots,
the jigsaw slots back into a kind of pattern
and, as you walk, you meet yourself,
turning casually down the same street.

Achill

Red fuchsia bells
drip from wild hedges,
tiny yellow flowers
stud the brown turf,
and the inscrutable mountain
lights to green clarity
when the sun
puts a finger
on Achill.

Then the sea is a bath
of salty diamonds,
on its dimpled surface
crawl the dark caterpillar shapes
of oaring curraghs,
the beaches are white sand
and clean aquamarine
licks rocky teeth
smoothing to cream
on shingle.

A few hours and the sun's touch
becomes a claw
flailing city flesh
to a raw fever.

In the pub
the thin-skinned tourists
swagger at pool,
challenging the locals
in their clumsy sweaters,
the few wind-shaven men
who were deaf to the city's
siren song.
Nimble in their boats,
they now shuffle shyly
with their cues

and pot their own black.

Blind Colours

My eyes are in my fingertips:
I don't see black,
I feel a rich fuzz,
a sinking into fur,
and I hear my cat crooning,
feel her claws knead my flesh.

Yellow is loud first
and then soft, like a mother
calling her child,
or like the sun, hot on my skin,
then gentle at the day's end.

Puce is a sudden flush in my cheeks,
an ugly notion of exposure,
but crimson and vermilion
excite my lips,
and orange is a round temptation,
a juicy feast on my tongue.

Green settles me,
I feel smooth leaves
with their little hairs
like my own cheek;

white is empty and clean,
I sense the air whistle
in my mouth when I say it:
white, echoing
and lonely, white.

Blue is rich but cold:
there's a feel of endlessness
about it, like waves
which never stop;
but turquoise is mysterious
and languorous,
my mouth lets the word go

regretfully, and I think
of strange places,
exotic fragrances that I'll never know.

Grey is soft and wistful
like the quiet cry
of a tired animal;
brown is dependable
like the earth, which is soft
if I fall, smelling damp
and comforting, full of roots,
steadying things.

We Were Like Sisters Weren't We

I stifled in that room
on the edge of that double bed,
you in your red cotton gown
hugging the other edge.
Backs to each other
I could feel your burnished hair
warning me off, sparking on the pillow:
keep to your side!
Not that I was anxious to flail about,
my pudgy toe accidentally nudge
your cold huddled feet.
I was hot, I ripped off
my choking flowered flanellette gown,
pushed into my hand by our hostess, fussing.
It hissed to the ground and
I moved carefully, letting my flesh spread.
You were so far away,
yet I scarcely dared to turn over –
you might decide to turn at the same time;
then we would have to feign sleep face to face.
Because neither of us slept.
I sighed and rustled, so did you,
but it was too intimate
for the feints of words.
I itched and wriggled,
raw in my skin in that hot bed,
nervous of your red sprite body,
so slimly, ethereally there,
restless too, but not naked, not sweating.
I had thought nothing of our sharing
this bed, we were like sisters weren't we,
but I couldn't relax.
Barbed sisterhood, territorially alert,
anxious to avoid collision.
In the morning, gravel-eyed,
I heard your polite yawn,
quick nightgown-held hop out of bed
to the solitary relief of a hot bath.

Two Sculptures by Rodin

Jeune Fille au Chapeau Fleuri des Roses AND *Femme Accroupie*

I am suspended
between two figures:
the girl in her rosebud hat;
and the woman, naked,
clutching herself.
The girl's dark eyes
are round
in curiosity and distaste;
the woman's eyes are closed,
her drawn cheek
rests upon her bent knee,
her sex squats openly
between her bare feet –
she is hoping and suffering
in ways the girl has never
dreamt of

Husk

Emptied of adventure
we return from long days
to find a grey husk
clinging to the cornice –
a small, perfect bulb
with a hole at the top.

We detach it gently
with curious fingers,
our eyes straining
to peer inside the gauzy orb
at a small, pitted comb.

Our breath shudders
for an instant,
imagining a creature
lying sticky in its birth juice
unseen
in the small room.

Our only token
is the empty sack –
its outer whorl
already thinning;

we are left
with the delicate,
fibrous remains

of a birth,
or perhaps
an abandoned expedition

At Queen Medb's Cairn

They buried you upright.
Your friendly thighs
and capacious bladder,
all your largesse of limb
now lost
under a windscored heap of stone
which sits, like a button,
on the upturned belly
of Knocknarea.

As we climb to pay tribute
the mossy slopes trickle
with a gushing generosity
like your juices
after love;

the hilly stream
has hewn its little way
through rock and earth
like a miniature
of your bladder's waterfall
that delved the land.

At the summit
I struggle out of layers
to bare my buttocks
in the airy howl;

squatting with
a hesitant squirt
on the grey cairn,
a worshipper at the shrine,
a hopeful apprentice
of your ancient mighty wave.

Harvest

A flung stick,
and the children
stamp on green gourds
in the long-stemmed grass,
scrabbling out conkers,
squatting with their hoard
in the briars,
fingers pith-sticky and blackberryish.

In the field
mother stoops to cut wheat:
white-eared and yellow-throated
sheaves to garnish
the waiting church.

Late evening:
the men rattle to town
with trailers of grain
wind on their knuckles;
'If the dry holds up,'
dusty caps are scratched,
'If the bank holds off,'
wallets in shiny pockets
rub empty lips together;
magpies dart at yellow stubble,
and the church bell
tongues a warning:

they stiffen,
remembering a neighbour
tinkering with his baler,
his small sons
leaping at the wheel
nudging the engine
to wake and bite:
one child ran
to drown his heartbeats
crouching in the ditch,

the other hollered home;
but there was time
only for dying,
father's blunt hands
plucking at breaths,
dry leaves hissing in the graveyard.

The men close memory's shutter
and tramp to flickering kitchens;
evening sucks the last light,
dogs yelp at cars
in a hysteria which no-one checks;

tomorrow they will sing:
'All is safely gathered in.'

Butter

In the first glow
of my laying out
I am all smooth
and golden –
a rich taste
waiting to melt
on the right tongue.

Then the knives come.
Dipping and scavenging,
they seek an easier passage
for dry bread,
they nibble at my edges
and stab at my heart,
leaving me pockmarked;
smudged with crumbs.

My plundered parts
are gloated over, licked,
spread out thin
with careful scrapes,
or smeared in thick welts
by greedy takers.

My solid sunshine
creams down their throats
for the gentle swallow –
the ooze between the teeth.

Broken into oily bubbles
by the churning
of their innards,
I endure the slow journey
of reconstitution,
biding my time
as I fatten again
to choke their veins
and stop their blood.

Hands

Small-nailed seekers
stroke like the cheeks of cats,
press like the heels of divers,
glide, keeled with heat
along the landscape of skin –
swellings of muscle,
outcrop of bone –
fingers follow spine ridges,
knuckles knead
at the dough of buttocks,
thumbs dig shadow lines
down thighs,
palms pad the calves
before the end
of the nerve journey
at the feet.

There hot touches
link the heart,
tickle the liver,
lengthen the neck,
and all contained
on the foot's blind face,
turned up from down,

a cold creature
now glowing like a schoolgirl
after her first kiss.

Hands which spun
the soothing threads
of repose,
now part the pattern,
fold the fabric,
retreat and settle
further off;
blood tingles, quietens
to a low throb:
spent.

Mexico: Images

Quetzlcoatl, quiet serpent
and swooping bird,
when the solstice light
feathers down the angle
of the temple of the sun
you flicker into life,
sinuous and hungry.

At the mouth of the Jaguar dwelling
an obsidian heart
is nudged into my hand
by laughing pedlars,
a little black heart,
momento of red living ones
ripped out centuries ago
in the middle of these sleeping stones:
children, virgins, young men
fluting a different tune
for every step of death,
one for every foster family,
for every last suck of breath.

In the village
the faces are sober
at our bare-legged show,
and when we move to the musique tropicale
hands snake around us
reaching for crotches.

They call us the ballerinas,
the women won't look at us,
ashamed for our foolishness,
we retreat between our men –
the crowd writhes around us –
the black heart pumps
against my goosefleshed breast.

Pattern

Pain arrives,
on the slightest pretext,
making her home
in my belly –
a monthly visit is not enough.

I can feel her
hauling her bags
and hanging up clothes
inside me; the screech
of a chairleg
as she sits down.

The walls of my abdomen
lean in on her,
trying to force her out,
but only puncture
on her knitting needles.

She is fashioning
the story of my discontent,
drawing together the strands
into a bilious pattern,

some day she will slip
the finished garment on
and leave;

I will wear
the suffocating sleeve
long after memory
has sloughed off the encrustations
of outrage and regret –

pain has left her pattern
in my gut.

Diver

The silence
of a diver
preparing to plunge:

she holds her breath,
quivers, braces,
then falls
cleanly,
hands dividing the surface;

she finds the water's
hidden pocket,
stays wrapped
in its fold,
until bubbles
draw her up,
nose first,
on a rope
of ascending air.

The diver
is my voice
falling
into the liquid chambers
of your listening,

held
by the fastening
of your bright eyes.

When I emerge
new and buoyant,
I am a sudden
suck of air,
an arm rising,
borne
on the turning tide

Yosemite: Photo vs Memory

I recall
not the bald man's head
of the grey half dome,
forehead seamy
under the sky's blue tent,
nor our linked hands
around the fragrant, capacious waist
of the red sequoia,
not even the irreverent globes
of your naked behind;

because these have been
swallowed on the spot,
regurgitated in a new light
of struck poses,
the usurpers
of memory's tender,
wraith-shaped evocation

which traces the points of stars
on a furry-backed night sky,
scuffles at our secret thermal rill,
where black water was twin-tongued
with heat and molten ice,
the air large and effortless around us;
then our waking to frost
like loosening fingers
on the snug bags,
our nostrils keen with pine
and cool beginnings.

This is as it was,
and my black metallic eye
has left me
with cheap shots of the rest,
the guts of it all glossed over,
all flattened and forsaken.

Spider

I open my mouth
and out she crawls,
the spider who's been hiding
down the pipeline
of my gullet.
She comes hurrying
with long terrible legs.
She wants to build a trap.
She wants to bite deep,
leaving the mark
of a poisoned tooth.
She's been in the dark
too long, crowded
with the flushed down jetsam
of so many days.
Now she's out –
her black body
sharp against the light –
her purpose fails her.
She stays still, playing dead,
weighing up the options.
In the dark it was easy to nourish hate,
the crooked spaces
starved out forgiveness.
She looks at herself:
a furry body, delicate legs,
a mark like a shield on her back.
Then she feels it.
A strange, exciting push inside
to move, to find her place.
Marking her corner
she feels the rush of thread
spun by her humming innards
meet the air, sticky and silver.
Running against the breeze
she tacks her baseline
and settles to weaving,
touching the outflow
of her silent language.

In the Hazel Wood

I went out to the hazel wood
Because a fire was in my head
W.B. YEATS
'The Love Song of the Wandering Aengus'

The rain spilled its yearning
on the heavy branches
of the Hazel Wood.
Here the poet Yeats once dreamed
his pagan vision of the fleeting girl
whose fruits he chased
but never plucked,
until their taste left a bitter fur
on his middle-aged tongue.
Here the young man ranged
a thin black figure among the boles
tortured by mythologised desire,
and here we wait
for the shower to cease
its endless feeding
of the silver waters of Lough Gill.
As we watch,
the car windows go opaque
with whorls of steam,
our tongues and fingers
curl and tease, limbs liquefy
in the fond routine
of finding pleasure.
Our sighs outweigh the shower,
and, as we lie back
on flattened seats and button up,
the sun pierces through laden trees,
their gathered droplets
scattering in a gust
all golden in the light;
the lake shimmers a taut blue
and in the distance
a lone fisherman plies his boat
lit up in the sudden midday glow
after rain, his head dipping
towards the rainbow.

Balancing Act

I stand between two trees
measuring the distances
just as in childhood
I stood between parents
bisecting their separation.
A tender of the scales
I heaped more on the emptier side –
frantic for balance.

Now with you
I am at the other end
of the see-saw,
countering your down with my up,
your young with my old,
a past master of vice versa,
a juggler handing torches,
burning my fingers to make a circle.

Night Music
(for Liam)

Lake water
juggles the moon's reflection
into shimmering spheres
breaking and dissolving
on the shore.

The night
offers its hesitant overture:
lap and ripple
at our feet,
on our shoulders
a slow leak
from the dark cups
of leaves.

The sky is printed
with white fans of cloud,
pierced
by a bird's quick
reedy cry.

The wind sighs and settles
in the brittle arms
of the trees;
and faintly
a dog's lone howl
touches the single reach
of our listening.

Then, with your whistle
you conjure silvery notes
from the hills;
from lake end
to lake end,
echoes ride
on the air:
magic bubbles
breaking
on the horizon.

Friends (I)
(for Sydna)

Swimming
I see your brown arm angled,
your feet slowing churners,
your face pushing a fold of water,
then the sudden, vivid
whites of your eyes.
We laugh
at our full bodies
held so buoyant and weightless,
it is so with us,
even in cafes
or on the telephone:
a wavelet reaches
to meet a ripple,
both rounded and liquid —
arcs joining to form
a circle.

Friends (II)
(for Sarah)

You are a long-legged,
long-necked bird,
moving among grains and shingles,
dipping in the muted hollows.
When your feet wade the ebb-tide,
you feel the beat of distant breakers,
you delve for unseen creatures,
hiding in their sandy labyrinths,
the clouds tease your eyes
to probe beyond seamless edges.
Your careful movements
are sometimes broken
by a rolling, girlish run
towards a bright lure
in the fickle water.
I follow your ceaseless search –
your finds and disappointments –
it is the tracemark of my own.

Friends (III)
(for Clare)

We travelled together
laughing and marvelling,
you the more intrepid voyager,
small suitcase of yourself
moving to faraway waters,
your neat head, tail anchored
in some glimmering cave
before emerging again
into bands of light
to defy the sharks.

My seahorse:
I could ride
on the strength
of your convictions,
but the secret colours
of your fantasies
I can barely
imagine.

Watermelon Man
(a painting by Rufino Tamayo)

Watermelon man,
your curved melonslice grin
is pink as your namesake,
your crazy bashed old hat,
hunched shoulder and arm gripping yourself
as though chuckling inwardly,
a watermelon chuckle
trickling out of you
like sweet sticky juice;
you curve the ends of my black and white day,
my day of bleary head and blowsy self-pity
into a sticky pink smile
at myself and the world;
for here we are, cosy in my room,
alone together, shadowed by my lamp,
the chimes chink in the gusts outside,
my churning head is slowing,
taking a breath, and your
big brown pink-nailed hand
reaches across to me
and touches my lonely skin,
nudges my goosepimple ribs,
and I'm beginning to feel pink
with grins slicing all over me;
I'm a seed, a fruit, a luscious thing
snuggling in darkness, sticky with watermelon dreams.

Underneath Our Skirts

Although a temple
to honour one man's voluntary death,
his ceaseless weep of blood,
the women cannot enter
if they bleed --
an old law.

As the bridal couple glides
down the aisle,
her white veil twitching,
I feel my pains.
A woman
bleeding in church,
I pray for time,
for slow motion.
Unprotected, I bleed,
I have no bandage,
my ache finds no relief.
My thorns
are high heels
and itchy stockings.
He, the imitator, bleeds on
in numb eternal effigy,
his lugubrious journey of martyrdom
rewarded with worship.

Tonight custom demands more blood:
sheets must be stained
with the crimson flowers
of a bride's ruptured garden.
Her martyrdom
will be silent knowledge
suffered in solitude.

As we leave the house
of the male bleeder,
I feel myself wet and seeping,
a shameful besmircher of this ceremony
of white linen
and creamy-petalled roses;

yet underneath our skirts
we are all bleeding,
silent and in pain,
we, the original
shedders of ourselves,
leak the guilt of knowledge
of the surfeit
of our embarrassing fertility
and power.

Moon

A thumbprint
of smudged milk;

a cheekbone
climbing over
your scarf of irregular blues;

a bruised knee
pressed and puckered
while you bend.

Moon,
you show pieces
of yourself,
even in your
full disc
I sense
the rest of you
is hiding
in the dark,
a big woman
shy of her size,
showing a bare shoulder
or a coy toenail,

sometimes a face
shadowed and demure,
or roundly flushed;
Venus
the gem
on your quiet finger,
pointing our gaze
away

The Unravelling

I baulk at you
and want you,
and sew up the gaps
knotting the thread,
throwing back the wind's challenge.

But you open me
softly
when I'm not looking:
a dry sponge fills with water
with hopes
which can never be wrung;
these passages have blind endings,
my bold blood will falter,
back to the stitching,

but you're there
at the end of my seam,
and the unravelling
begins again.

Fountain

I am a fountain:
glittering, moving,
yet solid on the earth at base,
I spray myself about
and collapse back to rest
before the next burst.

Nobody points my movements
in the direction they want,
instead I dance roundabout
to my own tune,
and if others like it,
they come to watch the show.

They can listen to watery rhythms
which soothe them,
but I ask them not to muddy
my waters with their sweaty feet,
I can do so much, but not that;
they must keep a little distance,
let the sunlight warm my clean azure bottom.

The birds can sip my eddies,
their nimble beaks are friends,
and the leaves can bathe their ruddy faces,
while my prisms catch the moonlight
murmuring secrets in liquid code.

I pity the sturdy hose,
he can beat his way about,
yet if someone picks him up
he is their tool. I would give all his strength
for my gentle splendour, my pearly fingers
meeting in mid-air.

Love

Love turned fierce,
wore a bracelet of barbed wire
and said fie
to everyone but the lovers,
whose wide-eyed idyll
had spawned this committed guardian.
They sat together
wading in soft looks
while love went chopping:
she carved up the heart
of a lonely boy
who watched the murmuring heads
of the lovers –
she left him bleeding and lamenting,
wiping her knife on her skirt
she laughed
with terrible carelessness.

The lovers spoke dreamily of swans
and stars, and made their way
with tender tongues to bed;
love stood at their door
a flame-eyed sentinel,
her savage face
threw off all earnest visitors
in broken cartwheels
down the stairs.

For dinner Love consumed raw steaks
at her post,
the lovers nibbled chocolates
and earlobes,
and let night fall
languidly upon them.

Black Man

He wears his skin
like proud silk:
he is a jungle cat
in city clothes,
a flame
loosely bound
to a candle
and a candlestick.
He has stubby hair
which breathes
like his every pore
its own spicy perfume.
She wants him so bad
the white girl
in her beads and spectacles,
she leans in on him,
hardly breathing,
held in the thrall
of tender pink
on the insides of his lips –
the crunch of his teeth.
Like a moth
flirting with a flame,
she fancies herself
a plaything between
the wide, smooth hands
which she longs to see
on the pink, vulnerable inside,
which she longs to see
so dark on her pale body.
Flaccid and purposeless
her life, crying for depth,
her white bulk yearning
for a dark, fluid companion,
a prowling shadow
to follow her silently,
rounding out
the hidden silhouettes
of her throbbing dreams.

Ophelia

(after the painting by Millais)

I'm lying here
caught in the watery reeds
of sleep, but not yet drowned,
still trembling and moving,
conscious of myself struggling
after one thing or another.

Then there's the sound
of your heavy feet in my room,
your clumsy, tender solipsist's hand
which drags me gently by the hair
out of my half-won pool of slumber;

and I empty my eyes
to look through the watery darkness
at your pale round face,
floating incongruously in my night world,
wanting to be near me,
to pluck me from my own dreaming
into your dream,
the world you carry with you
even in the other, waking time.

My words are draggled,
nets pulling a heavy body,
and thoughts jerking into surface clarity
like hands slapping you hazily away.

Your face goes quiet before leaving me,
leaving both the dreams
torn and incomplete;
my sleep gone, I clutch at my cold limbs
and know that you clutch yours
in another room,
the broken leaves of our imaginings
swirling down the current,
and us on separate banks, shivering in the darkness.

The Climber

The climber clings to the indifferent stone
of the cliff, spume all around him
from the roaring descent,
which mocks his infinitesimal movements
yet cannot tear him into a furious
embrace towards death.

He is a slight man, this climber,
who would find himself atop the world
to feel its owner, or perhaps
the owner and tamer of his fears.

Everything is simplified, rarefied,
in the cool of rock and verticality,
his hands forcing a place for himself
in the snarling jags and pincers,
his toes pushing into the dumb resistance
of earth and stone,
his drenched face
and bright leaping eyes:

he will mount her finally
who makes to dash him from her breast,
his infant's yell of triumph
a trickle in the white deluge,

he will breathe easily,
resting so lightly
on soft green tufts,
his hands clenching
and unclenching her hair,
his blood singing him to silence –
rushing and beating,
inside and out –
the oldest melody.

Woman Solstice

On the longest day
head bursting with hidden thunder
I go to find icons.
I am bleeding
bruised red petals,
and thinking of old bones;
new cries.
The sheela-na-gigs
lie in a dank crypt
flanked by ogham stones
and carved shards,
tagged and crumbling.
The sheelas squat on shelves –
forgotten; defiant.
One opens her legs
in a glaze of red,
one mocks death
with a thick glare
and a thrusting tongue.
Another gives herself joy
with a finger
on her pleasure pulse.
Some are featureless,
breastless,
but all open knees
pulling wide labia
with large, insistent hands.

They dare the eye to recoil.

The longest day
throbs to an end
blue light fading slow;
as I watch the roll
of the moon's disc
behind gathering clouds,
I am lying on cool sheets
splay-thighed
and smiling.

I Haul Back

My words stay netted;
a shoal of fish
too wayward for release,
they bump and flip
in my veins.

I haul back fins
seeking your tongue
as a mesmeric dam;

when my lips journey your body
the trapped fish
moan in my throat,
they somersault
in a whirlpool
down to greet your entry,
they dance around you
with water-swallowed
silver-bellied shouts,
then quiver
in my fingers,
which dawdle the spicy caves
of your armpits;
their O mouths pop
sighs which hiccough
down the pink coral stairs
of my ribs.

If one escaped,
with its eager tail
and clumsy splash,
it might drench you
in the salty wave
of my passion,
a fish to be thrown back,
the prize unwanted,
the fisherman
unimpressed.

The Glove

Rain on the black window
like fingernails tapping the silence –
I'm here alone with my charm.
It lies beside me,
a temporarily abandoned glove,
ready to put on.
'Women are too charming,'
you said tonight. 'They aren't honest.'
Wearing my glove I say:
How would you like it without the charm?
You'd hate it.

My glove drops it all far away,
out into the long currents of rain
gleaming down the street.

Raging Wind

Astride the wind
my anger goes rampaging
with the sea, racing and spitting,
urging each other on
to slap down walls, sink boats,
seethe into hollows
and create quiet explosions.

I am left here, empty,
a weak pod split
and dried
in a small lighted room.
My mind fingers scenes
from the past,
like an old woman
muttering with her beads.

Buffeting and blustering
on the saddle of the wind
my anger pummels at your door,
sending her breath
into the cracks of your window,
rattling and moaning
to steal your sleep.

Her tongue slides
through your keyhole
whispering poisoned dreams
into your snoozing ear;

a great suck
accompanies her exit,
slamming your door in parting,
shaking the foundations
of your house,

you will wake,
fearful and sick,
dreading her howl

Muse/Medusa

(from a Greek statue in the Louvre)

Immense in granular stone,
her breasts push against her cold dress,
her belly and thighs
are round and solemn,
her feet big and easy in sandals.
She holds the face of man at her side,
like a player's mask,
her large fingers in his curls.
His mouth is wide
in some bodiless oration
animated by her listening, her support.
Yet one gentle turn of her head away
can turn the strutting hero to a mute,
then her blanket of hair
seems to spark at him like rising snakes:
is this the cunning nightmare
in her nurse's guise?
Oh muse, your monumental mother's clasp
cannot be trusted, you have the power
to snap his head off,
turn the sound off,
leaving him open-mouthed and frozen.
If only he didn't doubt you,
yet who can be sure
when the swelling milky breast
gummed by the feeding baby
might bite back with fiercer fangs?
Or so he fears. Later he will woo
the vision of fertile creativity
to feed his endeavour,
but his thoughts get snagged
on the spectre of Salome, darting amongst her veils:
the precious head a ball
juggled between two dimpled hands.

Party Man

I am a laughing sea-lion,
I thread the needle of your desire,
my dark, dimpled chin
breaks open like a fruit
to the white of my teeth:
the seeds of promise.

I am a red bow-tie,
I carry the song,
my tongue rasps and lilts,
tickles the ice in glasses;

I am a dancing sailor,
wind in your ear,
the spray from my lips
arcs towards you.

I am a blind pebble,
in the whirlpool,
swilling and falling
I drop to the depths
of dreamless roundness:
oblivion.

Attitude of Love

In the clear quiet
before morning,
I sit, pillow-propped,
my month's blood pumping
in the white moon curve
of my belly.

You lie
curled around me
in an attitude of love.
Your spread palm
is warm
on my pulsing flesh,
your ginger beard
nestled at my side.

You are tunnelling in dreams
on the other side of the world,
yet your hand lies constant
soothing the unquiet creature
inside me.

My loud breathing
sends your hand
gently up and down;
hand with its long fingers
and long hairs,
hand that is pink
and generous,
hand that, hours ago,
sent me spinning in a floodmelt;

now holding my pain
as the blood drums
on this difficult dawning.

Hunter

You're a hunter
sending your weasel in
after my rabbit,
she's burrowing down to safety
hiding from you.

You fill me and dry me
and scathe me,
I'm parched with you, I'm withered –
my petals will fall
and the thorns will out.

You send your cormorant –
a strangled neck –
to catch my fish
as trophies,
You take my riches home
for boast meat.

I am left with the polluted ooze
of your motor boat,
the thin cry of the bloodied rabbit –
your pellets lodge deep
and fester.

A Wild Night

A wild night
of tantrum winds
and the broken glimmer
of stars,
the moon's butter-melt face
hiding
in a dark hood of cloud.
I dream you
along furtive streets,
find you waiting
at each corner,
your body light
against the wind.
My steps
eat the distance
to home,
and I miss
your standing at the door,
your warm hands
as I fumble inside
fringed with streamers
of cold.
I set out
the night's work,
and you dwindle
to a handsome footnote
beckoning with a tiny wink
beneath my busying thoughts.
Then the door
shoves my heart
back to beating,
and out of the night
you emerge,
as new and strange
as if the moon
had suddenly donned
an anorak
and arrived
on my doorstep.

Making Terms

In this new place
I have to make terms:
cupboard doors jab my head,
the table bites at my hip,
the wardrobe steps on my foot,
as we make our awkward dance
around the room.
My open window throws in
the elusive vowels of new voices –
they pass me by
like anonymous runners –
then, as I sip tea,
and breathe the new air
with more trust,
a song plunges in,
from the red wink of the stereo,
your face daubs the walls,
my green silk dressing-gown
tells me how you looked in it
that night; my clock bleats the hours
that we talked, delaying
until grey fish clouds nosed the dawn,
even my breasts turn traitor,
crying how your lips
said goodbye, and then goodbye,
lingering over each –

I duck between strange sheets
to darkness, a clean empty smell.

At the Spa

There's an old brown man
in black trunks
and a bruised hat;
he wades to his place
in a ripple of poplar leaves,
and the water's lips take him,
licking clean the lines.

His face opens out
like paper pulled smooth;
he adjusts the hat
to a jaunty peak,
his bare brown shoulders
straightening, leaning back.

Half a world away
a young brown man
angles at his blonde date
in the Marin jacuzzi;
piped water froths
on her taut thighs,
her hands perch on the edge,
her golden head well clear.

His flexed muscles glisten
as he foosters
at recalling the game; his prize
her bronze, motionless shoulders.
The chlorine-scented water
bleats a modulated serenade.

At Sárospatak
the brown man
drinks the shooting sulpher water
from a plastic cup.
A woman with a lapsed tummy
engages him:
he stands, hip rakish,
she grins, gap-toothed and easy –
the water slaps them gently
into life.

Autumn

The mountain lays out her red hair,
brown undercurls and limegreen tassles
scarlet-tipped and flaring.

She poses before a backdrop of pure lapis,
the jagged defiance of the Gothic castle
her stone tiara, its fluted shafts of window
sheer to her copper beech brows.

Stop and listen – the silence is her withheld breath,
she's watching the day fall like a dry gold leaf,
as the cowbells die on the waiting air,
and the liverspots grow on her poplar lemon skin;

as a woman sifts through fragrant apples,
only to find an acrid intruder
hiding beneath their plump cheeks,
bruised and sunken, like a toothless mouth.

The Potters' House

The potters move like shy dancers,
pouring tea into glossy cups,
serving crimson apples and slow jazz.
Terracotta vases and teapots
queue beside their warm kiln
like shivering women
waiting for the sauna.

Cats skitter in the garden,
following me to the outhouse
where I pee before an audience
of brindled fur and curious claws;
air is clammy on my skin,
wild ducks gather in dark fragments
on the hunched grey back of the river.

I open their door again,
this time to a waft of coconut,
a crackle from the red-rimmed stove
and comfortable twilight
beneath low ceilings.

The potters are quiet:
their agent clacks the gate,
his spider legs scuttle
into the nest of his car.
Theirs is a tenuous hold
on the underside of the leaf –

when I go a vase is put into my hands
dressed in paper folds,
like a child
wrapped against the wind.

First Autumn Night
(for Martin)

On the first autumn night
I open my window,
looking for your flame
to roar into me
from beyond the moon's
pearl-cool gaze.

My nostrils reach
for your smell
from the leaf-damp air;
your white, flaring laugh
from the mottled rustlings
in the eaves,
but the night toad squats, unmoved,
his fat throat
flickers dark green –
he has swallowed the sun.
His dank hide
eclipses your face,
the trees sweep you away
with their weary arms
like the last of summer.

I turn in
to my doll-yellow room,
where pieces of you dart
unfinished and awry –
your head a sunflower,
(blue birds, your eyes),
your firefingers on my skin,
the hot caprice of your tongue,
the eager blaze of your sex,
your long thigh
ember warm on mine –

I pull you around me
like a golden skin,
like a patched blanket
in the first autumn chill.

Old Women's Summer

Old women are moving
up and down the town,
like plump nuthatches
they bend to salvage
the heads of sunflowers
thrown in corners like pitted skulls,
they sit beside
fat bags of seed,
their fallen mouths
mumble over husking,
black kerchiefs in the honey noon.

In the market
old women are selling
veined purple beans,
the spotted globes of eggs
and windfall pears,
they offer Othello grapes:
'Sweet as pure sugar,'
dark as their eyes
in a trellis of wrinkles.

In the graveyard
old women tend the last beds
of their errant husbands,
paths are strewn with chestnuts
bursting from the pith
of spiny green shells,
the undergrowth flames out
like the flick of red petticoats
as the women swing carefully
onto the black skeletons
of their bicycles,
hands rooted, faces up
to greet the white glove
of the new season.

The Hungarian Sailor

He's a perverted jew, from a place in Hungary...His name was
Virag, the father's name that poisoned himself. He changed it by
deed poll, the father did.
JAMES JOYCE
Ulysses

At Szilvásvárad
he darted between branches,
hunting trout
in the quick and hover
of the stream,
found trout pools
with their flash and fin,
turn and snub;
then the waterfall –
a little garrulity
over moss-browed stone.

His splashes starved the water,
there was never enough:
Lake Balaton's breath
soured by German boats,
old fishermen idling
by the Chain Bridge,
hooking at some dream
of freedom, the coast
briefly held,
the lost territories,
the shrunken centre.

He felt his veins stiffen
like the deserted beds of rivers,
so he turned to the anonymous seas,
a wandering flower,
another father of Bloom,
his thoughts still rutted on the home patch,
the motionless, earth-held plate.

A bachelor of sixty,
sun-whipped like gargoyle driftwood
and beached
on a stranger shore,
he lets flow the trickly dew
of his own water:
going home.

No Nest

The stork
will not build her nest
on your chimney,
folding her white wings of luck
on your shelter,
though you have built it
carefully enough –

brick on red brick,
greenfooted ivy
torn from the bright window,
the kitchen scrubbed
to a grainy pile,
the shelves nailed up
for your mauve pottery,
the new fridge
so tenderly wiped
with the softest cloth,
and no air breathes;

the door is pulled close
on the two of you
in your matching chairs,
her tears sliding out
and no white cloth to wipe them,
no tender, absorbent word,
his eyes cleaving to a book,
the radio cackling
as in an empty shell,
her head full of the sound
of smothered birds,
of a stone rattling down
the dry chimney.

Auschwitz

Auschwitz:
sounds like a mouth
empty of hope
falling
to the death hush.

It's that hush
which today's birds
can't sing through;
the tourist shuffle
remove.

The earth is replete
with your lost flesh.

In the prisons
you built for yourselves
lie the left behind things:
the toothless brushes,
loll-tongued children's boots
pots past their prime,
a room full of your suitcases –
locked hopes from the old life
left unopened.

You are never more present
than in these possessions
that ink the outline
of your lives:
the piles of cracked shoes
recall your naked limbs
in the pits –
your swathes of hair
fill a room –
they took everything of you,
saved it for us,
whose tears cannot deflect
the accusatory lenses
of your broken spectacles.

Börzsony Hills

Past the walled village,
rutted cobbles,
and yellow twin-spired church,
we nose into the hills
to traces of snow
on brown undergrowth.

Our feet hesitate
on unrouted ground,
raised branches in our path,
wine bells of Christmas roses
collared in frost.

Then there's a sudden break and run
of boar, snouts up,
trotters marking the path
as their hairy bodies
lurch past the skinny boles
of hill trees in winter.

Stilled and silenced,
we listen
until the last sound
is our breath
on the white air

These Last Days

I cartwheel like a knife
into the sagging canvas of now –
it's a strange underwater dance,
all weed and drift –
my arrow nose shafts through
hunting you.

Like a whirlwind
coning down,
I'm peeling the brittle skin
of these last days
without you;

only in your arms
will I slowly open
the moist, seeded centre.

Notes

QUEEN MEDB'S CAIRN
Medb was the great warrior queen of Connacht. Her daring escapades and earthy, larger-than-life personality are to be found in Celtic literature and legend. Her stature is more like that of a pagan fertility goddess.

MEXICO: IMAGES
Quetzlcoatl is a Mexican god, part serpent and part bird.

WOMAN SOLSTICE
The summer solstice was associated with female energy in pagan times. Sheela-na-gigs are medieval carvings of women exposing their genitals. They were carved on churches and castles as a protection against evil spirits. They are kept in the crypts of the National Museum.

AT THE SPA
Marin county is a wealthy suburb of San Francisco, California.

OLD WOMEN'S SUMMER
This is the popular term for autumn in Hungary.

THE HUNGARIAN SAILOR
In Joyce's *Ulysses*, Leopold Bloom's father is a Hungarian Jew named Lipoti Virag, from Szombathely, who commits suicide in Ireland.

NO NEST
In Hungary it is considered a sign of good luck if a stork builds its nest on your chimney.